Chicago Bears Fun Facts

Trivia Ape

Published by Trivia Ape, 2023.

CHICAGO BEARS FUN FACTS

First edition. August 21, 2023.

Copyright © 2023 Trivia Ape.

ISBN: 979-8223092889

Written by Trivia Ape.

Also by Trivia Ape

50 States Trivia
Kansas City Chiefs Trivia Book
Chicago Bears Fun Facts
Green Bay Packers Fun Facts
Kansas City Chiefs Fun Facts
Minnesota Vikings Fun Facts
Denver Broncos Fun Facts
Detroit Lions Fun Facts
Las Vegas Raiders Fun Facts
Los Angeles Chargers Fun Facts
Pittsburgh Steelers Fun Facts

Table of Contents

Team History and Origins

- The Chicago Bears were originally founded as the Decatur Staleys in 1919 by A.E. Staley, a food starch company owner.
- The team moved to Chicago in 1921 and became the Chicago Staleys for one season before adopting the "Bears" moniker in 1922.
- The Bears are one of the NFL's two charter franchises, along with the Arizona Cardinals.
- The decision to rename the team to the Bears was to reflect baseball's Chicago Cubs, where they played their first season in Chicago.
- Chicago's first NFL game was a 20-0 shutout over the Moline Universal Tractors in 1920.
- The Bears have won a total of nine NFL Championships, with their most recent being Super Bowl XX in 1986.
- The team's mascot, Staley Da Bear, is named after the original Decatur Staleys.
- Soldier Field, the Bears' home stadium, opened in 1924 and has been their home since 1971.
- The "Monsters of the Midway" nickname originally referred to the University of Chicago's football team but was later adopted by the Bears.
- In 1940, the Bears set a record by defeating the Washington Redskins 73-0 in the NFL Championship Game, the most lopsided game in NFL history.
- The 1940s Bears teams were powered by the revolutionary T-formation, which is a basic formation in modern football.
- George Halas, one of the NFL's founding fathers, co-founded the Bears and coached them for 40 seasons in four stints.
- The Bears' iconic "C" logo was introduced in the 1960s and has been a staple on their helmets ever since.
- The team's fight song, "Bear Down, Chicago Bears," was penned in 1941 after a win.
- Chicago played the first-ever NFL playoff game in 1932, defeating the Portsmouth Spartans indoors at Chicago Stadium due to severe winter conditions.

● The Bears have had 28 different home stadiums in their history, more than any other NFL team.

● The club's colors – navy blue, burnt orange, and white – have been consistent throughout their history.

● The 1985 Bears are often considered one of the best NFL teams ever, finishing 15-1 and winning Super Bowl XX.

● The Bears' rivalry with the Green Bay Packers is the oldest in the NFL, beginning in 1921.

● The team's mascot during the 1920s was a live bear cub from the Lincoln Park Zoo.

● In 2006, the Bears won the NFC Championship, but lost Super Bowl XLI to the Indianapolis Colts.

● The Bears have made the playoffs 27 times in their storied history.

● Chicago played its 1,000th game on November 18, 2010, against the Miami Dolphins.

● The Bears have retired 14 jersey numbers, the most in the NFL.

● Chicago was the first NFL team to hold regular training camps.

● The Bears hold joint training camp practices with the Denver Broncos on occasion.

● They were the first team to implement daily practice sessions.

● The 1963 Bears defense recorded an NFL-leading 36 interceptions.

● Chicago's first-ever draft pick was Art Buss in 1936.

● The Bears were the first NFL team to have their games broadcast on radio.

● In the 1930s, the Bears were known for barnstorming across the country, playing exhibition games to promote the sport.

● The team's original colors were actually blue and orange stripes.

● In 1977, Walter Payton set the then single-game rushing record with 275 yards.

● The Bears were the first team to win 700 regular-season games.

● Chicago was the first club to purchase a player, buying Ed Healey from Rock Island for $100 in 1922.

● The Bears hold the record for the most entries into the Pro Football Hall of Fame.

● George Halas served the team in some capacity for 63 years.

● The Bears won back-to-back titles in 1932 and 1933.

• Chicago's 1942 team went undefeated in the regular season but lost in the championship game.

• The Honey Bears cheerleading squad cheered for the team from 1976 to 1985.

• In the 1937 NFL Draft, the Bears selected #1 overall, picking Sam Francis.

• The Bears' first-ever game at Wrigley Field ended in a tie.

• Chicago was the first team to hold a public practice under lights.

• The Bears made their first playoff appearance in 1932.

• Chicago played its first night game in 1922.

• The team's highest-scoring game was in 1965, beating the San Francisco 49ers 61-20.

• The Bears played in the first game broadcast nationally on the radio in 1924.

• Chicago's all-time leading scorer is placekicker Robbie Gould.

• The Bears won eight NFL titles before the Super Bowl era began.

• Chicago once had back-to-back shutouts in the playoffs in 1985.

Hall of Fame Players

- Walter Payton, nicknamed "Sweetness," rushed for a then-NFL record 16,726 yards in his career.
- Middle linebacker Dick Butkus was known for his ferocious play and was an 8-time Pro Bowler.
- Defensive end Doug Atkins stood at 6'8" and was an 8-time Pro Bowler.
- Mike Singletary, the leader of the 1985 Bears defense, was a 10-time Pro Bowl selection.
- Gale Sayers scored 22 touchdowns in his rookie season and had the nickname "The Kansas Comet."
- Brian Urlacher, the modern face of the Bears' defense, was inducted into the Hall of Fame in 2018.
- Bill George, a 1960s linebacker, is credited with inventing the middle linebacker position.
- Dan Hampton played both defensive end and defensive tackle and was part of the 1985 Super Bowl-winning team.
- Sid Luckman, a quarterback, led the Bears to four NFL titles and was a pioneer of the T-formation.
- Red Grange, the "Galloping Ghost," was one of football's first big stars in the 1920s.
- Richard Dent, Super Bowl XX MVP, recorded 137.5 career sacks.
- Bulldog Turner was a versatile player, playing center and linebacker, and was named All-NFL for seven consecutive years.
- Bronko Nagurski was a powerful fullback and linebacker who's considered one of the most versatile players in history.
- Stan Jones was a seven-time Pro Bowl offensive lineman known for his weightlifting regimen.
- Jim Finks, though primarily known as an executive, played quarterback for the Bears in the 1950s.
- George Blanda played 26 seasons in the NFL, starting with the Bears, and played both quarterback and kicker.
- Clyde "Bulldog" Turner played both offense and defense and was a 4-time NFL champion with the Bears.

• George McAfee was a dynamic halfback and defensive back known for his speed.

• Mike Ditka, better known as the coach of the '85 Bears, was also a Hall of Fame tight end for the team.

• George Connor was a 5-time All-Pro offensive lineman and linebacker.

• Joe Fortunato was a linebacker for the Bears in the 1950s and 60s and went to five Pro Bowls.

• Ed Healey was one of the NFL's first great linemen and was traded to the Bears for $100.

• William Roy "Link" Lyman was a 4-time All-Pro defensive lineman in the 1920s and 1930s.

• George Trafton, center for the Bears in the 1920s, was known for his rough play.

• George Musso, a guard and tackle, was the heaviest player of his era.

• Danny Fortmann was a 3-time All-Pro guard in the late 1930s and early 1940s.

• George Halas, while primarily known as a coach and owner, also played end for the Bears.

• Willie Galimore was a star halfback in the late 1950s before his tragic death in a car accident.

• Paddy Driscoll was a quarterback and halfback in the 1920s and was also a successful coach.

• Ed Sprinkle, nicknamed "The Meanest Man in Football," was a fierce defensive end.

• Harlon Hill was a standout wide receiver in the 1950s and won NFL MVP in 1955.

• Johnny Morris is the Bears' all-time leader in receptions.

• Bob Wetoska was a standout offensive lineman in the 1960s.

• J.C. Caroline was a cornerback and halfback in the 1950s and 60s.

• Doug Buffone was a long-time linebacker and fan favorite.

• Mike Hartenstine was a consistent and durable defensive lineman in the 1970s and 80s.

• Otis Wilson was a key linebacker on the 1985 championship team.

• Gary Fencik holds the team record for career interceptions.

• Steve McMichael was a key defensive tackle on the 1985 team.

● Dave Duerson was a Pro Bowl safety and part of the Super Bowl XX winning team.

● Keith Van Horne was a stalwart offensive lineman in the 1980s and 90s.

● Neal Anderson succeeded Walter Payton at running back and had a successful career.

● Jimbo Covert was a standout offensive tackle in the 1980s.

● Dennis Gentry was a versatile running back and kick returner.

● Willie Gault was a speedy wide receiver and key contributor on the 1985 team.

● Jay Hilgenberg was a 7-time Pro Bowl center in the 1980s.

● Kevin Butler is the Bears' all-time leading scorer among kickers.

● Tom Thayer was a consistent offensive lineman in the 1980s.

● Gary Lyle was a standout safety in the 1970s.

● James "Big Cat" Williams was a fan-favorite offensive lineman in the 1990s and 2000s.

Notable Coaches, General Managers and Front Office Personnel

• George Halas served as the head coach of the Bears for 40 seasons, winning six NFL Championships.

• Mike Ditka, a former Bears player, led the team to their only Super Bowl victory in the 1985 season.

• Lovie Smith was the head coach of the Bears from 2004-2012 and led them to Super Bowl XLI.

• Jim Finks served as general manager from 1974-1982, building the core of the 1985 Super Bowl team.

• Bill Tobin was a key executive in the 1980s and 90s, helping assemble talent for the Bears.

• Dave Wannstedt served as head coach from 1993-1998, succeeding Mike Ditka.

• Dick Jauron was the head coach from 1999-2003 and led the team to a division title in 2001.

• Phil Emery served as general manager from 2012-2014.

• Ryan Pace became the general manager in 2015 and was responsible for drafting key players like Roquan Smith and David Montgomery.

• Matt Nagy took over as head coach in 2018, bringing an offensive philosophy to the team.

• Mark Hatley was vice president of player personnel from 1998-2001.

• Ted Phillips has been the team's president and CEO since 1999.

• Jerry Angelo served as the general manager from 2001-2011.

• Rod Marinelli served as defensive coordinator from 2010-2012 and was known for his aggressive defensive schemes.

• Vic Fangio was the team's defensive coordinator from 2015-2018, creating one of the NFL's top defenses.

• Buddy Ryan, the architect of the famed "46 Defense," was the defensive coordinator for the 1985 Super Bowl team.

• Greg Blache served as defensive coordinator from 1999-2003.

• Ron Rivera, who later became a successful head coach, was the team's defensive coordinator from 2004-2006.

- John Fox, a former head coach for the Carolina Panthers and Denver Broncos, coached the Bears from 2015-2017.
- Chuck Pagano took over as the defensive coordinator in 2019 after Vic Fangio left.
- Ed McCaskey served as team chairman and had a significant influence on the organization.
- Virginia Halas McCaskey is the principal owner of the Bears and has been involved with the team for decades.
- George McCaskey currently serves as the team's chairman.
- Michael McCaskey served as the team's president and CEO from 1983-1999.
- Gary Crowton served as the team's offensive coordinator in the early 2000s.
- Terry Shea had a short stint as offensive coordinator in 2004.
- Bob Babich served as the team's defensive coordinator from 2007-2009.
- Mel Tucker was the defensive coordinator from 2013-2014.
- Adam Gase, later a head coach in the NFL, was the team's offensive coordinator in 2015.
- Dowell Loggains served as offensive coordinator from 2016-2017.
- Mark Helfrich, former head coach at Oregon, was the offensive coordinator in 2018 and 2019.
- Jack Pardee, a former Bears player, also served as the team's head coach in the 1970s.
- Abe Gibron was the head coach from 1972-1974.
- Neill Armstrong served as the head coach from 1978-1981.
- Paddy Driscoll, besides being a former player, also coached the team in the 1950s.
- Luke Johnsos co-coached the team with Hunk Anderson after Halas left for World War II service.
- Hunk Anderson, like Johnsos, was a co-coach during the World War II years.
- Clark Shaughnessy, a football innovator, was an assistant coach under Halas.
- Mike Murphy was an important assistant coach under Ditka.
- Bob Wetoska, a former player, also had a stint in the team's front office.

- Jim Dooley, another former player, served as head coach from 1968-1971.
- Ralph Jones was head coach in the early 1930s and introduced the T-formation, which revolutionized football.
- George Allen, a Hall of Fame coach, began his coaching career with the Bears.
- Harry Hugasian was an executive and scout for the Bears for nearly three decades.
- Bill Osmanski, a former player, also served in various roles in the front office.
- Sid Luckman, after his playing days, had roles in the Bears' front office.
- Jim Parmer was a long-time scout and executive for the Bears.
- Jim LaRue was an assistant coach under several Bears head coaches.
- Brad Childress, known for his time with the Vikings, was an offensive assistant for the Bears.
- Chris Tabor has been a long-time special teams coordinator for the team.

Draft History

- The Bears selected Sid Luckman with the 2nd overall pick in 1939. He would become one of the greatest quarterbacks in NFL history.
- In 1965, the Bears drafted Dick Butkus and Gale Sayers in the first round, arguably the team's most successful draft.
- Walter Payton, one of the greatest running backs in NFL history, was a first-round pick by the Bears in 1975.
- The Bears had no first-round pick in 1978, but they selected future Hall of Famer Dan Hampton in the 4th round.
- In 1983, the Bears selected Jimbo Covert, a crucial part of their Super Bowl-winning offensive line.
- The team picked Mike Singletary in the 2nd round in 1981, and he would become one of the game's top linebackers.
- The Bears drafted Brian Urlacher in 2000, who played his entire career in Chicago and entered the Hall of Fame.
- In 2017, the Bears traded up to select quarterback Mitchell Trubisky with the 2nd overall pick.
- The 1983 draft class was significant for the Bears, bringing in seven players who would contribute to their 1985 Super Bowl win.
- Despite their storied history, the Bears didn't draft a quarterback in the first round between 1951 and 2017.
- In 2018, the Bears snagged linebacker Roquan Smith in the first round, who quickly became a defensive star.
- The team drafted Devin Hester in 2006, and he would set multiple NFL return records.
- In 1984, the Bears drafted guard Tom Thayer, a local product from Joliet, Illinois.
- Alshon Jeffery was a 2nd-round pick by the Bears in 2012 and quickly emerged as a top receiver.
- Charles Tillman, a cornerstone of the Bears' defense in the 2000s, was a 2nd-round pick in 2003.
- The team selected Matt Forte in the 2nd round of the 2008 draft, and he became a key offensive player.

- In 2016, the Bears drafted Jordan Howard in the 5th round, and he rushed for over 1,000 yards in his rookie season.
- The Bears took Neal Anderson in the first round of the 1986 draft as the successor to Walter Payton.
- Mark Bortz, an 8th-round pick in 1983, switched from defensive to offensive line and became a two-time Pro Bowler.
- In 1991, the Bears selected defensive tackle Chris Zorich in the 2nd round, a Chicago native and fan favorite.
- The team took tight end Greg Olsen in the first round of the 2007 draft.
- David Terrell, drafted 8th overall in 2001, unfortunately, didn't live up to his high draft status.
- The Bears traded away their 2019 and 2020 first-round picks in the deal to acquire Khalil Mack.
- Curtis Enis, the 5th overall pick in 1998, struggled with injuries throughout his short career.
- In 2012, the Bears drafted Shea McClellin, expecting him to be a pass-rushing star, but he struggled to find a consistent role.
- Kyle Long, drafted in the first round in 2013, quickly became a standout offensive lineman.
- Cody Whitehair, a 2nd-round pick in 2016, became a reliable starter on the offensive line.
- Eddie Jackson, a 4th-round pick in 2017, emerged as one of the NFL's top safeties.
- The Bears drafted two Hall of Famers in the first round of the 1965 draft but didn't have another pick until the 10th round.
- In 2000, the Bears had two first-round picks and used them on Brian Urlacher and Mike Brown.
- Otis Wilson, a member of the famed 1985 defense, was a first-round pick in 1980.
- In 1993, the Bears selected Chris Gedney, who became a community ambassador for the team after his playing days.
- The team took Marty Booker in the 3rd round in 1999, and he became their top receiver for several seasons.
- Anthony Thomas, drafted in the 2nd round in 2001, won the NFL Offensive Rookie of the Year award.

- In 1990, the Bears selected safety Mark Carrier in the first round, and he made the Pro Bowl as a rookie.
- The team took Lance Briggs in the 3rd round of the 2003 draft, and he became a seven-time Pro Bowler.
- The Bears selected wide receiver Johnny Knox in the 5th round in 2009, and he made the Pro Bowl as a rookie.
- In 2019, running back David Montgomery was selected in the 3rd round and quickly established himself as a key player.
- The Bears have historically emphasized drafting defensive players, with many becoming long-time starters.
- James Daniels, an offensive lineman drafted in 2018, has shown versatility by playing both guard and center.
- Nathan Vasher, a 4th-round pick in 2004, set a then-NFL record with a 108-yard missed field goal return.
- The team selected defensive tackle Tommie Harris with the 14th overall pick in 2004, and he made three Pro Bowls.
- In 1988, the Bears selected Brad Muster in the first round, and he became a versatile fullback.
- The 2006 draft brought key players like Devin Hester and Danieal Manning to bolster the Bears' special teams and secondary.
- In 1999, the Bears selected quarterback Cade McNown with the 12th overall pick, but he struggled in the NFL.
- In 1994, the Bears drafted defensive tackle Jim Flanigan, who went on to have a productive career with the team.
- The Bears took tight end Desmond Clark in the 6th round in 1999, and he became a consistent target for several seasons.
- In 2015, the Bears selected Kevin White with the 7th overall pick, but injuries derailed his career.
- The team took William Perry in the first round in 1985, and he became a cultural phenomenon.
- In 1979, the Bears drafted Hall of Fame defensive lineman Dan Hampton with the 4th overall pick.

Offensive Star Players

● Walter Payton, nicknamed "Sweetness," is the Bears' all-time leading rusher with 16,726 yards.

● Sid Luckman led the Bears to four NFL championships during his tenure.

● Gale Sayers, despite a short career due to injuries, made a significant impact and is remembered for his elusiveness.

● Jim McMahon was the starting quarterback for the Bears' 1985 Super Bowl-winning team.

● Matt Forte ranks second in team history in rushing yards and is known for his receiving skills.

● Mike Ditka, before becoming the Bears' head coach, was a star tight end for the team.

● Brandon Marshall, although with the Bears for just three seasons, set several team receiving records.

● Neal Anderson succeeded Walter Payton as the team's starting running back and ranks third in rushing yards.

● Johnny Morris, a wide receiver in the 1960s, led the NFL in receiving yards in 1964.

● Curtis Conway was a reliable receiver for the Bears in the 1990s.

● Jay Cutler is the team's all-time leader in passing yards and touchdowns.

● Willie Gault was a key deep threat for the 1985 Super Bowl team.

● Harlon Hill, a receiver in the 1950s, won the NFL MVP in 1955.

● Tom Waddle became a fan favorite in the early 1990s for his gritty play at wide receiver.

● George Blanda, before his long tenure as a kicker, played quarterback for the Bears.

● Marty Booker, a wide receiver in the early 2000s, had two stints with the team and made the Pro Bowl.

● Thomas Jones was the leading rusher for the 2006 team that reached the Super Bowl.

● James "Big Cat" Williams was a cornerstone of the Bears' offensive line in the 1990s and 2000s.

- Olin Kreutz, a center, was a six-time Pro Bowler and a leader on the offensive line.
- Devin Hester, although primarily a return specialist, also contributed as a wide receiver.
- Doug Atkins, primarily known as a defensive end, occasionally played on the offensive line.
- Bob Wetoska was a key offensive lineman during the 1960s.
- Rick Casares was the team's leading rusher before Walter Payton and played in the 1950s and 1960s.
- Brian Piccolo, whose career was tragically cut short by cancer, was immortalized in the film "Brian's Song."
- Alshon Jeffery was a top receiving target during his tenure and set the team record for receiving yards in a season.
- Raymont Harris was a key running back for the Bears in the 1990s.
- Keith Van Horne was a long-time starting tackle for the Bears.
- Jordan Howard set the Bears' rookie rushing record in 2016.
- Stan Jones, an offensive lineman in the 1950s and 1960s, was inducted into the Hall of Fame.
- Rashaan Salaam, although his career was short-lived, won the NFL Offensive Rookie of the Year in 1995.
- Kellen Davis, a tight end, contributed during the 2010s.
- Matt Suhey was a fullback and Walter Payton's primary blocker during the 1980s.
- Jim Harbaugh, before his coaching career, was a first-round pick and quarterback for the Bears.
- Beattie Feathers, in the 1930s, became the first player in NFL history to rush for over 1,000 yards in a season.
- Kyle Long was a seven-time Pro Bowler at guard.
- Bobby Douglass, a quarterback in the 1970s, was known for his running ability.
- Anthony Morgan, a receiver in the 1990s, was known for his speed.
- Tarik Cohen, a running back and return specialist, earned a Pro Bowl nod in 2018.
- Mark Bortz, a guard, was a two-time Pro Bowler and member of the 1985 Super Bowl team.

- Dave Duerson, primarily a safety, occasionally played on offense.
- Ron Rivera, before his coaching career, occasionally played on offense despite being a linebacker.
- Brad Muster was a versatile fullback in the late 1980s and early 1990s.
- Dennis Gentry was a reliable running back and return specialist in the 1980s.
- Bill Wade, a quarterback, led the Bears to the 1963 NFL Championship.
- David Terrell, a wide receiver, was a top-10 draft pick in 2001.
- Roland Harper, a running back, played alongside Walter Payton and contributed significantly in the 1970s.
- Tom Thayer was a guard on the 1985 Super Bowl-winning team.
- Noah Herron, a running back, was a key contributor in the mid-2000s.
- Curtis Enis, a running back, was a first-round pick in 1998.
- Greg Olsen, a tight end, was a first-round pick in 2007 and contributed significantly before being traded.

Defensive Star Players

.Mike Singletary, nicknamed "Samurai Mike," was a key linebacker for the 1985 Super Bowl team.

● Dick Butkus is often regarded as the most intimidating linebacker in NFL history.

● Richard Dent, a defensive end, was the MVP of Super Bowl XX.

● Brian Urlacher, a middle linebacker, was the face of the Bears' defense in the 2000s.

● Dan Hampton, a defensive lineman, was inducted into the Hall of Fame in 2002.

● Charles Tillman, a cornerback, was known for his "Peanut Punch" to force fumbles.

● Otis Wilson, a linebacker, was a member of the 1985 Super Bowl team.

● Doug Atkins, a defensive end, was known for his size and strength.

● Steve McMichael, a defensive tackle, was a key player on the 1985 Super Bowl team.

● Gary Fencik, a safety, is the team's all-time leader in interceptions.

● Lance Briggs, a linebacker, played alongside Brian Urlacher and made seven Pro Bowls.

● Donnell Woolford, a cornerback, was a first-round pick in 1989 and had a successful career with the Bears.

● Bill George, a middle linebacker, is considered one of the pioneers of the position.

● Ed O'Bradovich, a defensive end, was a key player in the 1960s.

● Dave Duerson, a safety, was a four-time Pro Bowler and part of the 1985 Super Bowl team.

● Mark Carrier, a safety, made the Pro Bowl as a rookie in 1990.

● Adewale Ogunleye, a defensive end, was a key pass rusher in the 2000s.

● Tommie Harris, a defensive tackle, made three Pro Bowls during his tenure with the Bears.

● Eddie Jackson, a safety, has been a standout player since being drafted in 2017.

- Trace Armstrong, a defensive end, started his career with the Bears and was a consistent pass rusher.
- Joe Fortunato, a linebacker, was a five-time Pro Bowler in the 1950s and 1960s.
- Doug Buffone, a linebacker, played 14 seasons with the Bears.
- Mike Hartenstine, a defensive end, played 12 seasons with the team.
- Roosevelt Taylor, a safety, was a key player in the 1963 NFL Championship team.
- Wilber Marshall, a linebacker, was a key component of the 1985 Super Bowl team.
- Alan Page, although more known for his time with the Vikings, played for the Bears towards the end of his career.
- Leonard Floyd, a linebacker, was a first-round pick in 2016 and showed great potential.
- Corey Wootton, a defensive end, is remembered for recording the sack in which Brett Favre played his final snap.
- Chris Harris, a safety, had two stints with the Bears and was known for his hard hits.
- Nathan Vasher, a cornerback, set the then-record for the longest missed field goal return in 2005.
- William Perry, although also used on offense, was primarily a defensive tackle and a member of the 1985 Super Bowl team.
- Akiem Hicks, a defensive end, has been a key player for the Bears' defense in recent years.
- Kyle Fuller, a cornerback, was a first-round pick in 2014 and has been a standout player.
- Hunter Hillenmeyer, a linebacker, was a consistent contributor in the 2000s.
- Shaun Gayle, a safety, had a long tenure with the Bears and was part of the 1985 Super Bowl team.
- Mike Brown, a safety, was known for his game-changing interceptions.
- Jerry Azumah, a cornerback and return specialist, made the Pro Bowl in 2003.
- Alex Brown, a defensive end, was a key pass rusher for the Bears in the 2000s.

- Danny Trevathan, a linebacker, has been a leader on the defense since joining the team.
- Vince Evans, although primarily a quarterback, sometimes played on defense.
- Jim Osborne, a defensive tackle, played 13 seasons with the Bears.
- Richard Dent, in addition to his Super Bowl MVP, ranks as the team's all-time sack leader.
- J.C. Caroline, a cornerback, played 10 seasons with the Bears and made the Pro Bowl.
- Robbie Gould, although a kicker, made a game-saving tackle in a playoff game.
- Otis Wilson, in addition to his Super Bowl ring, was known for his pass coverage skills.
- Tim Jennings, a cornerback, led the NFL in interceptions in 2012.
- Ron Rivera, although more known as a coach, was a linebacker on the 1985 Super Bowl team.
- Mike Richardson, a cornerback, was a key player on the 1985 Super Bowl team.
- Warrick Holdman, a linebacker, was a key contributor in the early 2000s.
- Pernell McPhee, a linebacker, was known for his pass-rushing skills during his time with the Bears.

Team Milestones

- The Chicago Bears were founded in 1919.
  - Originally, the team was known as the Decatur Staleys.
  - In 1922, they officially became the Chicago Bears.
  - The Bears won their first NFL championship in 1921.
  - The team clinched back-to-back championships in 1932 and 1933.
- They have a total of 9 NFL Championships, with their most recent being Super Bowl XX in 1985.
  - The Bears have appeared in two Super Bowls: XX and XLI.
  - The 1940s were a dominant era for the Bears, winning 4 championships in that decade.
  - The "Monsters of the Midway" nickname originated during their dominant periods in the 1940s.
  - In 1963, under Coach George Halas, the Bears won their 8th NFL Championship.
  - The 1985 Bears defense is widely regarded as one of the best in NFL history.
  - The team celebrated its 100th season in 2019.
  - Chicago has appeared in over 35 playoff games throughout its history.
  - In 1940, the Bears recorded the most lopsided victory in NFL history, beating the Washington Redskins 73-0.
  - The Bears' famed T-Formation offense revolutionized football in the early 1940s.
  - "Bear Down, Chicago Bears" became the team's fight song in 1941.
  - The team had a 16-game unbeaten streak during the 1933-34 season.
  - In 1984, Walter Payton broke Jim Brown's rushing record while playing for the Bears.
  - The Bears were the first NFL team to have an indoor training facility.
  - They were also the first team to hold daily practices.
  - In the 1965 draft, the Bears had two of the top three picks.
  - The 2006 Bears reached the Super Bowl under Coach Lovie Smith.
  - Chicago holds the record for most members inducted into the Pro Football Hall of Fame.

- The Bears have retired 14 jersey numbers, the most in the NFL.
- They have won 20 division titles throughout their history.
- The Bears have had 27 playoff appearances as of 2021.
- The team's longest win streak is 17 games, spanning from 1933-34.
- The Bears have had four seasons with a perfect home record.
- In 2001, the Bears had an impressive 13-3 season after finishing 5-11 the previous year.
- The team has played in over 1,400 games.
- The Bears have had ten or more wins in a season over 25 times.
- They've finished first in their division more than 20 times.
- Chicago Bears were one of the charter members of the NFL.
- The team holds the record for most entries into the NFL's All-Decade Teams.
- In 1932, the Bears played in the first-ever indoor NFL game.
- They were also part of the first-ever televised NFL game in 1939.
- The Bears have had three undefeated seasons, though they were shorter seasons.
- They are one of the two remaining franchises from the NFL's founding in 1920.
- In 1965, Gale Sayers scored 6 touchdowns in a single game.
- The Bears were the first team to win 700 official games.
- They clinched their 700th win against the Tampa Bay Buccaneers in 2015.
- The Bears have had back-to-back winning seasons multiple times.
- They've also had back-to-back-to-back winning seasons more than once.
- The team has been part of some of the coldest games in NFL history.
- Chicago has had over ten 10-win seasons in a single decade.
- They've recorded more than 20 shutouts in a single decade.
- The Bears have had multiple 6-game win streaks in their history.
- They have a storied rivalry with the Green Bay Packers, making it the longest in the NFL.
- The Bears have won multiple games with a margin of over 50 points.
- They were the first team to record a safety in the Super Bowl.

Franchise Records

● Walter Payton holds the record for most rushing yards in franchise history with 16,726 yards.

● Mike Ditka has the most receiving touchdowns for a tight end in team history.

● Brian Urlacher holds the team record for most tackles.

● Devin Hester holds the NFL record for most non-offensive touchdowns.

● Jay Cutler is the Bears' all-time passing leader.

● Richard Dent has the most sacks in team history.

● Charles Tillman set the team record for defensive touchdowns.

● Matt Forte holds the franchise record for most receptions by a running back.

● The 1985 team holds the record for most points scored in a season.

● The 1932 team allowed the fewest points in a season.

● Robbie Gould is the franchise's leading scorer.

● Gary Fencik holds the team record for most career interceptions.

● The 2001 Bears have the team record for most takeaways in a season.

● The 1985 Bears defense scored 5 touchdowns, a franchise record.

● Olin Kreutz has played the most games as a Bears center.

● The 1942 team holds the best regular-season record at 11-0.

● The Bears' longest field goal was 58 yards, made by Paul Edinger.

● Sid Luckman holds the franchise record for most passing touchdowns in a game with 7.

● Bill Wade holds the record for most passing touchdowns in a season.

● George McAfee holds the franchise record for most punt return touchdowns.

● Eddie Jackson has the most defensive touchdowns in a single season.

● The 2012 Bears defense holds the record for most interception return touchdowns in a season.

● Jim Harbaugh holds the record for most consecutive pass attempts without an interception.

● Walter Payton has the most 100-yard rushing games in franchise history.

- The 1985 Bears hold the record for the largest margin of victory in a Super Bowl.
- Willie Gault holds the team record for most kickoff return yards.
- The Bears have the most Hall of Famers in NFL history.
- Walter Payton holds the record for most carries in a season.
- Devin Hester has the most punt return touchdowns in a season.
- The 1941 team holds the record for most consecutive games won.
- The 1985 Bears defense allowed the fewest points in a 16-game season.
- Matt Forte holds the franchise record for most yards from scrimmage.
- Johnny Morris holds the team record for most receptions in a season.
- Mike Brown holds the franchise record for most overtime touchdowns.
- The Bears scored the most points in a game with 73 against the Washington Redskins.
- Walter Payton has the franchise record for most total touchdowns.
- The 1985 team holds the record for most sacks in a season.
- Devin Hester holds the franchise record for most total return touchdowns.
- The 2006 Bears scored the most touchdowns in a season.
- Doug Plank holds the team record for most fumble recoveries.
- Otis Wilson holds the franchise record for most sacks in a playoff game.
- Walter Payton has the most multi-touchdown games in team history.
- The 1941 team holds the record for most shutouts in a season.
- The 1984 Bears have the franchise record for most rushing touchdowns in a season.
- The 2006 team holds the record for most total yards in a season.
- The 2001 Bears had the most interception return yards in a season.
- Walter Payton holds the team record for most seasons leading the team in rushing.
- The 2012 team holds the record for most blocked kicks returned for touchdowns.
- The 2006 Bears had the most kickoff return touchdowns in a season.
- Richard Dent holds the franchise record for most career forced fumbles.

Stadium History and Stadium Facts

- The Chicago Bears originally played their games at Wrigley Field.
  - In 1971, the Bears moved to Soldier Field.
  - Soldier Field underwent a major renovation and reopened in 2003.
  - Despite the renovation, Soldier Field retained its historic colonnades.
  - The stadium is located near Lake Michigan, offering a scenic view.
  - It is the oldest NFL stadium in operation.
  - Soldier Field has a seating capacity of over 61,000.
  - The stadium has been designated as a Chicago Landmark.
  - It has hosted a variety of events including concerts, soccer matches, and even ice hockey games.
  - The Bears have hosted five NFC Championship games at Soldier Field.
  - In 2002, the final game before renovation saw the Bears play the Jacksonville Jaguars.
  - The field's natural grass is often a point of discussion for its condition, especially late in the season.
  - Soldier Field was named in honor of American soldiers who died in wars.
  - The stadium has been used for military training and drills in the past.
  - It has also been a venue for religious and civic events, including addresses by several U.S. Presidents.
  - Soldier Field's iconic columns are part of its original design from the 1920s.
  - The stadium has undergone several renovations, the most significant in 2002-2003.
  - The playing surface at Soldier Field has been replaced multiple times.
  - In 1984, Walter Payton broke Jim Brown's rushing record at Soldier Field.
  - The seating capacity has been reduced over the years, from over 100,000 in the 1920s to its current capacity.
  - The 2003 renovation was met with controversy, as many believed it compromised the historic integrity of the stadium.
  - Soldier Field was declared a National Historic Landmark in 1987.
  - The Bears have had numerous memorable moments at the stadium, including "The Fog Bowl" playoff game in 1988.

- The stadium hosted the opening match of the 1994 FIFA World Cup.
- Soldier Field was also the site of the first Special Olympics games in 1968.
- The columns at Soldier Field are lit up during night games, adding to the ambiance.
- Despite being the oldest stadium, its renovation makes it one of the most modern on the inside.
- Soldier Field's video boards were added during the 2003 renovation.
- The Bears share the stadium with numerous other events and teams, including the Chicago Fire FC.
- The stadium's design allows for maximum noise retention, giving the Bears a home-field advantage.
- Its proximity to downtown Chicago makes it unique among NFL stadiums.
- Soldier Field's design is considered a mix of classical and modern architecture.
- The Chicago Park District owns and operates Soldier Field.
- Parking can be limited, but the stadium is accessible via public transportation.
- The playing field at Soldier Field sits below street level.
- The stadium has been the site of several record-setting attendance events in its history.
- Soldier Field has a memorial water wall dedicated to war veterans.
- Tailgating is a popular tradition for Bears fans before games at Soldier Field.
- The stadium has hosted international soccer games, featuring teams like Brazil, Germany, and the USA.
- Soldier Field has also been a concert venue for bands like U2, The Rolling Stones, and Coldplay.
- The stadium has an underground heating system to prevent the field from freezing in cold conditions.
- "The Midway," named after the team's nickname "Monsters of the Midway," is the main concourse of Soldier Field.
- Soldier Field has multiple dedicated spaces and monuments honoring military personnel.

- The Bears' Pro Shop, located at Soldier Field, offers a wide range of merchandise.
- Several statues, including ones of Walter Payton and George Halas, were unveiled outside Soldier Field in 2019.
- The stadium's end zones are adorned with the team's colors and iconic "C" logo.
- Due to its location, high winds from Lake Michigan can sometimes affect gameplay.
- The 1988 "Fog Bowl" playoff game at Soldier Field is one of the most iconic games in NFL history.
- Over the years, Soldier Field has been known for its challenging turf conditions, especially during winter.
- The stadium's horseshoe design allows for a great view of the Chicago skyline from certain sections.

Playoff Moments

• The Bears have participated in two Super Bowls, winning one in the 1985 season.

• Their first Super Bowl win in Super Bowl XX was a 46-10 victory over the New England Patriots.

• In 2006, led by Brian Urlacher, the Bears made it to Super Bowl XLI but lost to the Indianapolis Colts.

• The 1940 Championship game saw the Bears defeat the Washington Redskins 73-0, which remains the most lopsided victory in NFL history.

• Their 1985 defense allowed only 10 points total in their three playoff games leading to the Super Bowl.

• The "Monsters of the Midway" defense in the 1980s propelled the Bears to multiple playoff appearances.

• The 1941 Championship game saw the Bears defeat the New York Giants 37-9.

• The Bears defeated the New York Giants 14-10 in the 1963 Championship game.

• Chicago's playoff run in 2010 ended in a heartbreaking NFC Championship loss to the Green Bay Packers.

• The 2018 Bears were defeated by the Philadelphia Eagles in a dramatic "double doink" missed field goal.

• The 1943 Championship game was another dominant win for the Bears, with a 41-21 victory over the Washington Redskins.

• The 1934 team lost to the New York Giants in the famous "Sneakers Game" where the Giants switched footwear for better traction.

• Walter Payton, one of the greatest running backs ever, unfortunately never scored a touchdown in a Super Bowl. His only Super Bowl appearance was in 1985.

• The 1986 Bears, following their Super Bowl win, returned to the playoffs but lost to the Redskins in the Divisional Round.

• Chicago's 1956 Championship game ended in a loss to the New York Giants.

- The 1988 Bears made it to the NFC Championship game but were again bested by the San Francisco 49ers.

- In 1990, Chicago was defeated by the eventual Super Bowl champions, the New York Giants, in the playoffs.

- The 2018 playoff loss was especially heart-wrenching as the Bears had a stellar 12-4 regular season.

- During the 2001 playoffs, the Bears were upset by the Philadelphia Eagles in the Divisional Round, despite a 13-3 regular season record.

- Their 2010 NFC Championship loss was especially bitter as it came at the hands of their long-time rivals, the Packers.

- Chicago defeated the New Orleans Saints 39-14 in the 2006 NFC Championship game to reach Super Bowl XLI.

- The 1942 Bears went undefeated in the regular season but were upset by the Redskins in the Championship game.

- During their 2006 Super Bowl run, the Bears defeated the Seattle Seahawks 27-24 in an intense overtime Divisional game.

- The 1984 Bears made it to the NFC Championship but were defeated by the 49ers.

- Chicago's 1946 Championship win came against the New York Giants with a final score of 24-14.

- The 1932 Bears won their first league title in an indoor playoff game against the Portsmouth Spartans.

- The Bears' 2010 Divisional Round win was against the Seattle Seahawks, with a decisive score of 35-24.

- During the 1979 playoffs, Walter Payton ran for 106 yards against the Philadelphia Eagles, though the Bears lost.

- The 1933 Bears won the NFL Championship by defeating the New York Giants 23-21.

- The 1985 Bears' playoffs included a shutout victory against both the Giants and the Los Angeles Rams.

- In 1987, the Bears again made the playoffs but were defeated by the Redskins in the Divisional Round.

- The 1956 Bears made it to the NFL Championship but were bested by the New York Giants.

- The Bears' 1940 team shut out the Washington Redskins in the most lopsided playoff game in history.
- In 1941, the Bears clinched the Championship title with a solid win over the Giants.
- The 1943 Bears secured another title by defeating the Redskins.
- In 1963, the Bears defense shone in a tight victory over the Giants to claim the Championship.
- The 1977 Bears made the playoffs but were defeated by the Dallas Cowboys.
- The Bears' 1986 playoff journey ended with a loss to the Washington Redskins.
- In 1991, the Bears' playoff hopes were cut short by the Dallas Cowboys in a tight game.
- The 2005 Bears won the NFC North but were defeated by the Carolina Panthers in the Divisional Round.
- Chicago's 1994 playoff run ended with a loss to the San Francisco 49ers in the Divisional Round.
- The Bears defeated the New Orleans Saints in the 2006 NFC Championship during a snowy game at Soldier Field.
- Chicago's 2018 team lost to the Philadelphia Eagles in the Wild Card round due to the infamous "double doink" missed field goal.
- The Bears' 1946 team clinched the Championship title with a solid win over the Giants.
- In the 1934 Championship, the Bears were bested by the Giants, who wore sneakers for better grip.
- The 1942 Bears had a perfect season but lost to the Washington Redskins in the Championship game.
- Chicago's 2010 team defeated the Seattle Seahawks to advance to the NFC Championship.
- The Bears' 1956 playoff run ended with a loss to the Giants in the NFL Championship.
- The 1984 Bears reached the NFC Championship but were defeated by the San Francisco 49ers.
- Chicago's 2018 season ended with a heart-wrenching loss to the Philadelphia Eagles in the Wild Card round.

Player Jersey Numbers

- The Bears have retired the number 34 in honor of Walter Payton, one of the greatest running backs of all time.
- Mike Ditka's number 89 is one of the numbers retired by the Bears.
- Linebacker Dick Butkus is remembered by his number 51, which is retired by the franchise.
- The iconic number 40 was worn by Gale Sayers, and it is also retired by the team.
- Sid Luckman, the legendary quarterback, wore number 42, which is no longer in use.
- The great linebacker Brian Urlacher donned the number 54 throughout his career.
- Red Grange, known as "The Galloping Ghost," wore the number 77.
- Number 66 is retired in honor of Clyde "Bulldog" Turner.
- The number 50, worn by Mike Singletary, is another number that's been retired by the Bears.
- George McAfee, who wore number 5, is among the Bears' greats who have had their numbers retired.
- The number 3 is retired in honor of Bronko Nagurski.
- Devin Hester, known for his explosive returns, wore the number 23.
- The recent Bears star Khalil Mack dons the number 52.
- Mitchell Trubisky, the former Bears quarterback, wore number 10 during his time with the team.
- The number 65 was worn by guard Tom Thayer, a key member of the 1985 Super Bowl team.
- William "Refrigerator" Perry, known for his size and surprising agility, wore number 72.
- The iconic number 7 was worn by George Halas himself during his playing days.
- The number 33, worn by Charles Tillman, became synonymous with the "Peanut Punch" to force fumbles.
- Allen Robinson, a standout receiver for the Bears in recent years, wore number 12.

- Danny Trevathan, a vital part of the recent Bears' defense, wears number 59.
- Eddie Jackson, the star safety, dons the number 39 for the Bears.
- Number 15 was worn by wide receiver Brandon Marshall during his time with the team.
- Jim McMahon, the quarterback of the 1985 Super Bowl team, wore number 9.
- The number 71 is associated with the legendary defensive end, Alex Brown.
- Matt Forte, a standout running back for the Bears, wore number 22.
- Olin Kreutz, the long-time center for the Bears, wore number 57.
- Number 35 was worn by Neal Anderson, another great Bears running back.
- Number 80 was donned by wide receiver Curtis Conway.
- The number 63 was worn by standout center Jay Hilgenberg.
- The number 26 was associated with Tim Jennings, a cornerback known for his interceptions.
- Linebacker Lance Briggs wore the number 55 throughout his illustrious career with the Bears.
- Anthony Miller, a wide receiver for the Bears, wore number 17.
- The number 83 was worn by tight end and wide receiver, Martellus Bennett.
- Johnny Knox, known for his speed at wide receiver, wore number 13.
- The number 96 was donned by defensive end, Akiem Hicks.
- Number 18 was worn by wide receiver Darnell Mooney.
- The number 44 was associated with Nick Kwiatkoski, a linebacker for the Bears.
- Eddie Goldman, a defensive tackle, wears number 91.
- The number 38 was worn by safety Adrian Amos during his time with the Bears.
- Number 58 was donned by Roquan Smith, a standout linebacker for the team.
- The number 21 was associated with Major Wright, a safety for the Bears.
- Kyle Long, a standout offensive lineman for the Bears, wore number 75.
- The number 16 was worn by wide receiver, Pat Dunsmore.

• Leonard Floyd, a former first-round pick for the Bears at linebacker, wore number 94.

• Number 45 was associated with fullback J.P. Darche.

• Tarik Cohen, known for his agility and playmaking abilities, wears number 29.

• The number 20 was worn by safety Craig Clemons.

• Number 97 is associated with Willie Young, a defensive end for the Bears.

• The number 11 was worn by wide receiver Josh Bellamy.

• Kevin White, a former first-round pick for the Bears at wide receiver, wore number 13.

Ownership History

- The Chicago Bears were founded by George Halas and Dutch Sternaman in 1920.
- Originally named the Decatur Staleys, the team was initially owned by the Staley Starch Company.
- George Halas bought the rights to the team in 1921 and moved them to Chicago.
- The team was renamed the "Chicago Bears" in 1922 to reflect the city's baseball team, the Cubs.
- The Halas family has owned the Bears for multiple generations. George "Mugs" Halas Jr. took a leadership role after his father.
- Currently, Virginia Halas McCaskey, the daughter of George Halas, is the principal owner of the Bears.
- George Halas served multiple roles over his tenure: player, coach, and owner.
- Under the ownership of the Halas family, the Bears have won a total of nine NFL Championships.
- The team has remained in the Halas family for over a century, a rarity in modern professional sports.
- George Halas's ownership saw the Bears become one of the most storied franchises in the NFL.
- Halas passed away in 1983, but his legacy continues through his family's ownership.
- The McCaskey family, descendants of Halas, have held onto the team, resisting several offers to sell.
- Brian McCaskey is the current Vice President of the Chicago Bears.
- George McCaskey, one of Virginia's children, is the current Chairman of the Bears.
- During the Halas ownership, the Bears have played in three different stadiums.
- The team played at Wrigley Field from 1921 to 1970 before moving to Soldier Field.
- Under the Halas/McCaskey ownership, the Bears have made 26 playoff appearances.
- Soldier Field underwent significant renovations in 2003, modernizing the iconic stadium.
- Despite various challenges, the McCaskey family has expressed a consistent desire to keep the team within the family.
- Virginia McCaskey, as of my last update in 2021, is one of the oldest owners in the NFL.
- The Halas and McCaskey family ownership has seen the team through multiple eras of football, from its inception to the modern NFL.
- Under their ownership, the team has boasted many Hall of Famers, from Walter Payton to Brian Urlacher.
- The Bears' ownership has placed a strong emphasis on community involvement and charity work in Chicago.
- They've also consistently stressed the importance of defense in the team's identity.
- Despite their long-standing ownership, the Halas/McCaskey family has hired various GMs and coaches to run football operations.

- The team's ownership has overseen the Bears during some of the most iconic moments in NFL history, including the 1985 Super Bowl win.
- The Halas legacy is honored by the team, with the initials "GSH" displayed on the team's jerseys.
- George Halas's influence extends beyond the Bears; he's often credited as one of the founders of the NFL.
- Under the McCaskey family, the Bears have emphasized maintaining the team's rich history and traditions.
- The ownership has faced criticism at times, but their commitment to the team and city has never wavered.
- The Halas/McCaskey ownership era has seen some of the greatest rivalries in sports, especially the Bears-Packers rivalry.
- George Halas's tenure as owner/coach saw him become one of the winningest coaches in NFL history.
- The Bears' ownership has remained uniquely stable in a league where team sales and relocations are not uncommon.
- The team's deep ties to Chicago are reflected in their ownership's commitment to the city.
- Soldier Field, the team's home since 1971, is a Chicago landmark and a testament to the team's storied history.
- The ownership has overseen the team through various challenges, from on-field struggles to off-field controversies.
- George Halas was known for his hands-on approach, often taking personal interest in players' well-being.
- The McCaskey family's approach to ownership has been more removed from day-to-day operations but still deeply involved.
- Over the years, the family has made difficult decisions in the team's best interest, from coaching changes to player acquisitions.
- While business aspects of the team have evolved, the family's love for football and the Bears remains constant.
- Under the Halas/McCaskey leadership, the Bears have been involved in many league-wide initiatives and changes.
- The team's ownership has played a role in shaping the NFL's policies and direction.
- Through the ups and downs, the family's dedication to the Bears' legacy has been a guiding principle.
- The Bears' ownership has emphasized player safety, especially in recent years as concerns about concussions have grown.
- The commitment to winning and excellence has been a hallmark of the team's ownership throughout its history.
- As of 2021, the McCaskey family has expressed no plans to sell the team, ensuring that the legacy of George Halas continues.
- The Halas/McCaskey era has seen the Bears become a global brand, with fans worldwide.
- Their ownership has contributed significantly to the NFL's growth and prominence.

● Soldier Field's renovations under their watch have ensured the stadium remains a modern venue while honoring its history.

● The Halas/McCaskey legacy is intricately woven into the fabric of the NFL, with the Chicago Bears at its heart.

Fanbase

- The Bears have one of the oldest fan bases in the NFL, stemming from the team's inception in 1920.

- "Da Bears" is a popular phrase among fans, popularized by a series of sketches on "Saturday Night Live."

- Bears fans are known for their passionate loyalty, even during the team's less successful seasons.

- Tailgating is a time-honored tradition among Bears fans, especially in the Soldier Field parking lots.

- The fanbase has its own fight song, "Bear Down, Chicago Bears," played after every touchdown.

- Fans often brave frigid temperatures to attend games, given Chicago's notorious winter weather.

- The term "Bear Weather" was coined by fans, suggesting the team plays better in cold conditions.

- The "Superfans" sketch on SNL, with characters like Bill Swerski, paid homage to the passionate Chicago fanbase.

- Many Chicago celebrities, including Barack Obama and Bill Murray, have publicly expressed their support for the Bears.

- Soldier Field often resonates with the chant "Defense! Defense!" a nod to the team's storied defensive history.

- Bears fans have a tradition of wearing team-colored orange and navy blue on game days.

- The "Monsters of the Midway" nickname, which fans often use, originally belonged to the University of Chicago's football team.

- The "Bearman" (Don Wachter) is a superfan known for attending games with a bear head hat.

- In 2006, when the Bears made it to the Super Bowl, the city of Chicago was adorned in Bears flags and colors.

- Bears fans have a longstanding tradition of throwing home parties during games, with Chicago-style pizza and hot dogs as staples.

- Many Chicago bars are dedicated Bears establishments, offering game-day specials and decked out in memorabilia.

- The fan base has an active online presence, with several fan websites, blogs, and forums.
- Tailgate recipes like "Da Burger" and "Bears Brats" have been passed down through generations of fans.
- Fans often commemorate legendary players by wearing their retired jersey numbers.
- The city of Chicago has witnessed multiple celebratory parades organized by fans after significant Bears victories.
- Soldier Field's seating capacity is over 61,000, and it's common for fans to fill the stadium, rain, or shine.
- Many fans still wear retro jerseys, honoring legends like Walter Payton, Dick Butkus, and Mike Singletary.
- The "Windy City Flyer," a nickname for Devin Hester, often had fans on their feet in anticipation of a kickoff or punt return.
- The tradition of training camp in Bourbonnais, IL, saw thousands of fans yearly attending practices.
- Many families have held season tickets for generations, passing them down and keeping the fandom alive.
- The team's 1985 Super Bowl win still remains a topic of fond memory among older fans.
- "Club Dub" became a fan-favorite term in recent years, representing the team's post-game locker room celebration.
- The Bears' mascot, Staley Da Bear, is a favorite among young fans.
- Throughout the NFL, Bears fans are known for traveling well and often making their presence felt in away stadiums.
- "Kissin' titti3s," a fun saying started by fans, became a viral sensation referencing quarterback Mitchell Trubisky.
- Radio broadcasts of games, especially with former announcers like Jim Durham, hold nostalgic value for many fans.
- Bears fans have a reputation for their vast football knowledge, often referencing historical plays and players.
- Many fans collect Bears memorabilia, from signed footballs to game-worn jerseys.
- It's a tradition for fans to boo the Green Bay Packers, the Bears' chief rivals, regardless of where they're playing.

- Fan festivals, like the "Bears 100 Celebration" in 2019, saw massive gatherings of fans and legends.
- The Bears' social media pages have millions of followers, indicating their vast online fanbase.
- Chicago's "Magnificent Mile" often lights up in Bears colors during the playoff season.
- The "Orange Out" games, where fans wear orange to Soldier Field, create an intimidating atmosphere for visiting teams.
- Fans have a love-hate relationship with the team's fight song, but almost everyone knows the words.
- Numerous podcasts and YouTube channels run by fans provide in-depth analysis of the Bears.
- Every NFL draft sees thousands of fans speculating and hoping for the team's next star player.
- Game rituals among fans include specific chants, songs, and even superstitions to bring good luck.
- Many Chicago businesses show support by offering Bears-related promotions during the football season.
- A popular fan saying is "In Pace We Trust," referring to General Manager Ryan Pace.
- Bears fans internationally often gather in dedicated bars or establishments to view games.
- The fan base is diverse, comprising fans of all ages, backgrounds, and from various parts of the world.
- Despite modern conveniences, many fans still prefer listening to games on the radio, reminiscent of old times.
- Fans eagerly await the annual schedule release, planning trips and gatherings around game days.
- The Bears-themed cornhole game is a popular pastime during tailgates.
- Through highs and lows, the constant among the Bears has been their dedicated and passionate fanbase.

Rivalries

- The Bears-Packers rivalry is one of the oldest and most storied rivalries in NFL history.
- This rivalry began in 1921, and the teams have played each other over 200 times.
- The Bears and Packers are tied in the all-time series, showcasing the balance in this long-standing competition.
- The Vikings-Bears rivalry, part of the NFC North, has also been intense since Minnesota's entry into the NFL in 1961.
- The Detroit Lions, another NFC North team, have had their share of memorable battles with the Bears.
- The Bears' rivalry with the New York Giants dates back to the NFL's early years, with both teams being among the league's pillars.
- Chicago and Green Bay have both won multiple championships, adding to the gravitas of their matchups.
- The "Monsters of the Midway" versus the "Lambeau Leap" showcases the cultural difference in the Bears-Packers rivalry.
- Former Bears coach Lovie Smith once said that his primary goal was to beat Green Bay.
- Fans of both the Bears and Packers often engage in friendly banter, especially in cities close to the Wisconsin-Illinois border.
- The Bears-Cowboys matchups have also drawn significant attention, especially during the prime years of both teams.
- Games against historic teams like the 49ers and Steelers are always circled on fans' calendars.
- The 1985 Bears' victory over the Patriots in Super Bowl XX added a chapter to the Bears-Patriots inter-conference rivalry.
- While the rivalry with the Packers is the most intense, divisional games against the Lions and Vikings are also crucial.
- The Bears and Packers once met in the playoffs in 2011, a rarity adding fuel to their competitive fire.
- Legendary players like Walter Payton, Brett Favre, and Aaron Rodgers have been central figures in these rivalries.

- The rivalry games often have playoff implications, especially late in the season.

- Historic Lambeau Field and Soldier Field have been the primary battlegrounds for the Bears-Packers clashes.

- The Bears' rivalries have produced some of the NFL's most memorable moments, from incredible catches to defensive stands.

- The intensity of the Bears-Packers rivalry is such that families in the region often have split allegiances.

- The "Black and Blue Division" nickname for the NFC North signifies the physical nature of the rivalries.

- Both teams have legendary linebackers in their history, like Butkus for the Bears and Nitschke for the Packers.

- The Bears' competition with the Rams, especially in the early NFL days, was a significant rivalry.

- Matches against the Redskins, especially in the playoffs, have been significant in shaping the Bears' history.

- The Bears' rivalries are not just limited to the NFL. Before the merger, games against AFL teams also drew attention.

- The 1940s saw the Bears and Redskins face off in several crucial matches, including lopsided victories for Chicago.

- The intensity of the rivalries is such that records and stats often don't matter; any team can win on any given day.

- The media often highlights the Bears-Packers week, showcasing the significance of the match.

- The "Bears still suck" chant, popular among Packers fans, is an example of the banter between the fanbases.

- Brian Urlacher and Brett Favre's interactions on the field are some of the memorable moments in the Bears-Packers rivalry.

- Many players, upon joining the Bears, quickly realize the importance of games against Green Bay.

- There have been instances where players switched sides, like Julius Peppers moving from the Bears to the Packers.

- The rivalry games are always a hot ticket, often with inflated prices and sold-out stadiums.

- The atmosphere during these games, both in the stadium and the surrounding areas, is electric.
- The build-up to the rivalry games often starts weeks in advance, with fans and analysts making predictions.
- Legendary coaches like Vince Lombardi for the Packers and George Halas for the Bears have added depth to the rivalry.
- The Packers' cheesehead hats are often a source of humor and banter for Bears fans.
- The Bears and Packers have both had periods of dominance in the rivalry, making it even more balanced.
- The rivalry extends beyond just the games, with debates about cities, fanbases, and even cuisines.
- Former players from both teams often acknowledge the intensity and significance of the rivalry in interviews.
- Even during the preseason or non-competitive games, the desire to beat the rival team is evident.
- The games often feature hard tackles and intense physical play, living up to the "Black and Blue Division" name.
- The Bears-Packers rivalry has been featured in documentaries, showcasing its rich history.
- Many fans plan trips and vacations around the rivalry games, making it a central event.
- Social media amplifies the rivalry, with fans, players, and even official team accounts joining the banter.
- The Bears' rivalries have produced iconic NFL images, from snow-covered games to game-winning touchdowns.
- The respect between the teams is evident, even amid the fierce competition.
- The outcomes of the rivalry games often have significant implications on division standings and playoff scenarios.
- Freezing temperatures, especially in outdoor games at Lambeau and Soldier Field, add an extra layer to the rivalry.
- The legacy of the Bears' rivalries ensures that new chapters will always be added, keeping the history alive.

First Five Years

● The Chicago Bears were originally founded as the Decatur Staleys in 1920.

● In their inaugural year, the team was based in Decatur, Illinois, and was sponsored by the A.E. Staley food starch company.

● In 1921, the team moved to Chicago and became the Chicago Staleys.

● By 1922, the team was renamed the Chicago Bears, a name inspired by the Chicago Cubs, whose park they were sharing.

● The team's founder, A.E. Staley, handed the operational control to George Halas in 1921.

● Halas, besides being an owner, also played for the team and coached, making him a multi-faceted figure in the early days.

● The Bears claimed their first league championship in 1921.

● The team's early years were instrumental in boosting the popularity of professional football in the U.S.

● In an era dominated by ground games, the Bears were pioneers in emphasizing the forward pass.

● The Bears and the Cardinals (also based in Chicago at the time) quickly became fierce rivals.

● Red Grange, one of the era's biggest stars, joined the Bears in 1925.

● Grange's signing was a significant event, drawing massive crowds and helping legitimize the professional game.

● The team played its first game at Wrigley Field in 1921.

● George Halas's influence extended beyond the field; he played a crucial role in establishing the NFL's foundation.

● In 1924, the Bears finished with a 6-1-4 record, showcasing their early dominance.

● Joey Sternaman, brother of Chicago Cardinals owner Chris Sternaman, played for the Bears, adding a twist to the local rivalry.

● The team's early successes were built on a solid defense and innovative offensive strategies.

● The Bears, under Halas, were pioneers in integrating detailed film study into their preparations.

• In the first five years, the Bears played against teams like the Buffalo All-Americans, Rock Island Independents, and Dayton Triangles.

• The NFL was still in its infancy, and teams often played against non-league opponents. The Bears were no exception.

• The 1925 season saw the Bears go on a barnstorming tour with Red Grange, playing games in multiple cities in a short span.

• This tour played a crucial role in establishing the Bears (and the NFL) as a national brand.

• In their early years, the Bears' colors were not the iconic navy and orange but were instead blue and tan.

• George Trafton, an early Bears player, was known for his aggressive play and is considered one of the first great centers in NFL history.

• Dutch Sternaman, co-owner with Halas in the early years, was also a key player and coach.

• The Bears' early rosters had multi-sport athletes, showcasing the diverse talent pool of the era.

• While the forward pass was not as prevalent as it is today, the Bears were among the teams that embraced it earlier than most.

• Tickets for a Bears game in the 1920s cost as little as $1.

• The team's early successes set the foundation for Chicago becoming one of the NFL's cornerstone cities.

• The Galloping Ghost, Red Grange, had a significant impact, with some games drawing as many as 70,000 spectators.

• The NFL's first-ever playoff game in 1932 featured the Bears against the Portsmouth Spartans (later the Detroit Lions).

• While this game is just beyond the five-year mark, the buildup and importance began during the Bears' first five years.

• Halas's leadership style, both as a coach and owner, was hands-on, often leading practices and designing plays.

• The Bears in the 1920s often played multiple games in a week, a stark contrast to the modern NFL schedule.

• Early Bears games weren't just about football; halftime shows, including live bands, were a big draw.

• The team's initial logo was a bear running with a football, a simpler design compared to the modern "C" logo.

- In the pre-NFL draft era, the Bears' roster was built through local signings and acquisitions.
- The early Bears often played in leather helmets, without the face guards and visors seen in today's game.
- Halas's influence was so significant in the early NFL that he's often referred to as "Mr. Everything."
- The team's first five years laid the groundwork for the Bears becoming one of the NFL's "Original Teams."
- Despite facing financial challenges in the early years, the Bears' management remained committed to building a winning team.
- The team's move to Chicago was instrumental in its growth, with the city's large population providing a bigger fan base.
- Early game strategies revolved around power running and ball control, with occasional deep passes catching opponents off guard.
- The Bears' early history is a testament to the resilience and vision of its founders, especially George Halas.
- The team's initial days were filled with challenges, from convincing fans to watch games to ensuring player safety.
- While the play was rougher and rules were different, the passion and commitment to the sport were evident even in the 1920s.
- The Bears' initial successes set a winning culture that would define the franchise for years to come.
- The team's early growth was parallel to the NFL's growth, with both facing uncertainties but eventually succeeding.
- Chicago's rich sports culture, with baseball's Cubs and the emerging Bears, made it a hotspot for sports in the 1920s.
- The legacy of the Bears' first five years is evident today, with the team's storied history and passionate fan base continuing the traditions set in the roaring twenties.

Mike Ditka

- Mike Ditka was born on October 18, 1939, in Carnegie, Pennsylvania.
- He played both tight end and linebacker during his college football career at the University of Pittsburgh.
- Ditka was a first-round draft pick (5th overall) by the Chicago Bears in 1961.
- He was the first tight end to ever be inducted into the Pro Football Hall of Fame.
- Ditka was named the NFL's Rookie of the Year in 1961.
- Over his playing career with the Bears, he caught 316 passes for 4,503 yards.
- He was a five-time Pro Bowl selection during his playing career.
- Ditka also played for the Philadelphia Eagles and the Dallas Cowboys during his NFL career.
- He became the head coach of the Chicago Bears in 1982.
- Under Ditka's leadership, the Bears won Super Bowl XX in 1986.
- His coaching style was described as fiery and passionate.
- Ditka's iconic sweater vest became a fashion statement in Chicago during his coaching tenure.
- He also became known for his famous motivational speeches.
- Ditka is one of only two individuals to have won an NFL title as a player, an assistant coach, and a head coach.
- He was famously portrayed by actor George Wendt in several "Saturday Night Live" skits.
- Ditka has a restaurant named after him in Chicago.
- He became a television commentator after retiring from coaching.
- Ditka had a notable cameo in the film "Kicking & Screaming" as a youth soccer coach.
- He was the first tight end to catch over 1,000 yards in a single season.
- Ditka's number, 89, was retired by the Chicago Bears in 2013.
- In total, he scored 43 touchdowns during his playing career with the Bears.
- He's known for his outspoken nature, both on and off the field.
- Mike Ditka was inducted into the College Football Hall of Fame in 1986.

- During his coaching tenure, he had a win-loss record of 121-95.
- Ditka has been actively involved in various charity initiatives throughout his life.
- He also tried his hand at golf and participated in several PGA Tour celebrity events.
- Ditka has written several books, including his autobiography "Ditka: An Autobiography."
- He's been referred to as "Iron Mike" due to his tough and no-nonsense approach.
- Ditka is known for his memorable quotes, one being, "Success isn't permanent, and failure isn't fatal."
- He coached the New Orleans Saints after leaving the Bears.
- Mike suffered a heart attack during the 1988 season but recovered and returned to coaching.
- He has been an advocate for retired NFL players and their health issues.
- Ditka's aggressive coaching approach was instrumental in the development of the famous '46 Defense.'
- He played a total of 12 seasons in the NFL as a player.
- Ditka is of Ukrainian and Polish descent.
- He is a member of both the College Football Hall of Fame and the Pro Football Hall of Fame.
- As a coach, Ditka was known for his emotional outbursts on the sidelines.
- He's considered one of the most iconic figures in Chicago sports history.
- Ditka played himself in an episode of the popular TV show "Third Rock from the Sun."
- He was also a co-owner of the Arena Football League team, the Chicago Rush.
- Ditka is a devout Catholic and has spoken about his faith in various interviews.
- He was a three-time All-American during his college football days.
- Mike was one of the earliest tight ends to be used as a genuine receiving threat in the NFL.
- He was known for his strong blocking ability and aggressive playing style.
- Ditka had a short-lived self-titled TV show in the late 1980s.

● He has spoken about the challenges and pressures of coaching in a football-crazy city like Chicago.

● Ditka was known to have a strong bond with many of his players, including Jim McMahon and Mike Singletary.

● He has been honored with the "NFL Coach of the Year" award twice.

● Mike Ditka was a pioneer in utilizing the tight end position as an integral part of the offensive game plan.

● Even after his coaching days, Ditka remains a beloved figure in Chicago and is often sought after for his opinions on the Bears and football in general.

Walter Payton

- Walter Payton was born on July 25, 1954, in Columbia, Mississippi.
- Nicknamed "Sweetness," he was known for his smooth playing style and unmatched work ethic.
- Payton was drafted by the Chicago Bears in the first round of the 1975 NFL Draft.
- He spent his entire 13-year NFL career with the Bears.
- Walter set the NFL's all-time leading rushing record with 16,726 yards—a record that stood for 18 years.
- He was a nine-time Pro Bowl selection.
- Payton won the NFL MVP award in 1977.
- Despite his relatively small stature for a running back (5'10"), he was known for his powerful running style.
- Walter Payton passed away at the young age of 45 in 1999.
- He was inducted into the Pro Football Hall of Fame in 1993.
- Payton's number, 34, was retired by the Chicago Bears.
- He is often mentioned in debates about the greatest running back in NFL history.
- Walter was known for his signature "stutter-step" move.
- He also had a talent for throwing the ball and recorded several touchdown passes in his career.
- Payton was known for his tremendous off-field philanthropy.
- The NFL's "Man of the Year" award was renamed in his honor to the "Walter Payton NFL Man of the Year" award.
- He played college football at Jackson State University.
- Walter was an avid drummer and had a love for music.
- He also briefly raced cars after his retirement from football.
- Payton was known to run hills as part of his rigorous training regimen.
- He scored 110 rushing touchdowns in his career.
- Walter set a then-record by rushing for 275 yards in a single game in 1977.
- He was a key player for the Bears when they won Super Bowl XX.
- Payton's autobiography, "Never Die Easy," reflects his approach to life and football.

- He was known for his incredible fitness levels and rarely missed a game due to injury.
- Walter was also a successful entrepreneur and had several business ventures after retiring.
- He was known for his humility and often credited his offensive line for his successes.
- Payton had a unique pre-game ritual of eating licorice and refusing to drink water until after the game.
- He was a dedicated family man and often spoke about the importance of his wife and kids.
- Walter often wore a headband during games, which became part of his iconic look.
- He loved playing pranks on his teammates to keep the locker room atmosphere light.
- Even among other legends, Payton was often the player to watch during Pro Bowl games.
- He was known to avoid running out of bounds, preferring to take on tacklers.
- Walter's foundation, the Walter & Connie Payton Foundation, continues to make charitable contributions today.
- He was the youngest of three siblings and was particularly close to his brother, Eddie.
- Despite his achievements, he was famously left without a touchdown in Super Bowl XX, something he regretted.
- Payton held the Bears' record for most rushing yards in a season for over three decades.
- He was known for his incredible balance, often showcased in runs where he'd tip-toe along the sidelines.
- Walter was a dedicated mentor and inspired many young running backs, including his successor, Neal Anderson.
- He had a famous rivalry with Detroit Lions' running back Barry Sanders.
- Payton had a special relationship with Bears' head coach Mike Ditka.
- He also briefly tried his hand at broadcasting after retirement.
- Walter's son, Jarrett Payton, also pursued a career in football.

- He had an unmistakable high-pitched laugh that endeared him to fans and teammates.
- Walter's work ethic was legendary, with stories of him working out and running even during vacations.
- He was a fan of martial arts and incorporated them into his training routine.
- Payton was known to keep detailed notes and diaries about his games and performances.
- He believed in playing the game with respect and was known for helping up opponents he'd just run over.
- Walter was known for his resilience, often turning potentially negative plays into positive yardage.
- Payton's legacy is felt throughout Chicago, with numerous memorials, statues, and places named in his honor.

Bronko Nagurski

• Bronko Nagurski was born on November 3, 1908, in Rainy River, Ontario, Canada.

• His full name was Bronislau "Bronko" Nagurski.

• Nagurski was a massive player for his era, standing at 6'2" and weighing around 235 pounds.

• He played both fullback and defensive tackle for the Bears.

• Bronko was a key player for the Bears in the 1930s and played a pivotal role in their early success.

• He was a three-time NFL champion with the Bears.

• Nagurski was known for his incredible strength and toughness.

• He played college football at the University of Minnesota and was a standout there.

• Bronko was one of the inaugural inductees into the Pro Football Hall of Fame in 1963.

• He was also inducted into the College Football Hall of Fame in 1951.

• Nagurski's number, 3, was retired by the Chicago Bears.

• Legendary stories of his strength include him running into (and breaking) brick walls.

• In addition to football, Bronko had a successful career as a professional wrestler.

• He won the World Heavyweight Wrestling Championship multiple times.

• Nagurski's famous play in the 1932 NFL Championship Game involved a forward pass, a rare occurrence then.

• Bronko was known to have a gentle demeanor off the field, contrasting his on-field persona.

• He returned to the Bears in 1943 after a five-year hiatus and helped them win a championship.

• Nagurski ran a service station after his football and wrestling careers.

• His son, Bronko Nagurski Jr., also played football, notably in the CFL.

• The Bronko Nagurski Trophy is awarded annually to the top defensive player in college football.

- Despite playing in a leather helmet era, he was known for his ferocious tackling ability.

- Nagurski was an integral part of the famed "Monsters of the Midway" Bears teams.

- Stories about him often sound like tall tales, including knocking multiple opponents out of games.

- He was an All-Pro selection five times during his career.

- Bronko played a total of 97 games for the Chicago Bears.

- He's often cited in discussions about the most versatile players in NFL history due to his proficiency on both sides of the ball.

- Nagurski was known to play through injuries, exemplifying the tough nature of players from his era.

- He passed away in January 1990 at the age of 81.

- Bronko was of Ukrainian and Polish descent.

- His sheer size and power were unmatched in his time, making him a dominant force on the field.

- Nagurski is remembered for his famous quote: "I'm not mean, I just like to play football."

- In 1943, at the age of 35, he scored a touchdown in the NFL Championship Game.

- He's one of the few athletes to have succeeded at the highest levels in two different sports (football and wrestling).

- Nagurski's college exploits include once rushing for over 200 yards in a single game—a huge feat for the 1920s.

- His name is synonymous with early NFL history and its development into a popular sport.

- In his prime, he was one of the highest-paid athletes in America.

- Bronko was known for his humility and was often uncomfortable with his celebrity status.

- He remains a beloved figure in Chicago sports history.

- Nagurski was known to train rigorously, even by the standards of his time.

- His signing by George Halas in 1930 was considered a significant coup for the Bears.

- Bronko was known to be a loyal teammate and formed close bonds with many of his peers.

- He played in a time when the NFL was fighting for relevance against college football and other professional sports.
- Nagurski's style of play was instrumental in drawing fans and building the league's popularity.
- He played in the first-ever NFL game at Wrigley Field in Chicago.
- Despite his success, Bronko faced financial challenges after retiring and worked various jobs to support his family.
- In college, he was also a standout in basketball and track and field.
- His last game in 1943 marked one of the most impressive comebacks in sports history.
- Nagurski's enduring legacy is that of an athlete who, despite all odds, dominated in multiple realms.
- His wrestling bouts were as popular as his football games, drawing huge crowds.
- Bronko Nagurski remains a symbol of raw power, determination, and versatility in the sports world.

Sid Luckman

- Sid Luckman was born on November 21, 1916, in Brooklyn, New York.
- He played quarterback for the Chicago Bears from 1939 to 1950.
- Luckman was a crucial player in popularizing the T-formation in professional football.
- He led the Bears to four NFL Championships during his career.
- Sid was inducted into the Pro Football Hall of Fame in 1965.
- He set numerous passing records, many of which stood for decades.
- Before joining the Bears, he played college football at Columbia University.
- Luckman's number, 42, was retired by the Chicago Bears.
- He was named NFL MVP in 1943.
- Sid was a seven-time All-Pro selection.
- He was the first modern T-formation quarterback and changed the way football was played.
- Luckman passed for 7 touchdowns in a single game, a record at that time.
- He also served in the U.S. Merchant Marine during World War II.
- After retiring from playing, Sid had a successful business career.
- He also briefly served as a mentor and coach for young players.
- During his era, he was widely regarded as the best quarterback in the game.
- He's known for his six-touchdown game against the New York Giants in the championship.
- Sid was the son of German and Polish Jewish immigrants.
- He authored a book titled "Luckman's Passing" detailing T-formation strategies.
- In 1947, he had a career-high in passing yards with 2,712.
- Sid Luckman passed away on July 5, 1998.
- He was named to the NFL 1940s All-Decade Team.
- In total, he threw for 14,686 yards in his NFL career.
- He's often cited in discussions about the greatest quarterbacks of all time.
- Sid remains the Bears' all-time leader in several statistical categories.
- He was known for his intelligence and ability to read defenses.
- He had a strong arm and was known for his deep throws.

- Sid was one of George Halas' favorite players and trusted leaders on the field.
- His leadership qualities were evident even during his college days at Columbia.
- He was a multi-sport athlete in his younger days.
- Sid's record of 28 touchdown passes in a season stood for decades.
- He also had a stint as a sportscaster after retiring.
- Luckman was known for his training regimen and dedication to the game.
- His playoff performances are legendary, especially his 5 touchdown game in 1943.
- Sid was a significant figure in establishing Chicago as a dominant football city.
- He was known to be a gentleman off the field, respected by teammates and opponents alike.
- He played in 128 games for the Chicago Bears.
- Sid remains a revered figure in Bears' history.
- He played at a time when the NFL was still battling for mainstream popularity.
- Sid's style of play was instrumental in making the passing game a significant part of the NFL.
- He was known for his game preparation and studying opponent tendencies.
- Sid often mentored younger players, ensuring the team's continued success.
- He was a central figure during the Bears' dynasty years in the 1940s.
- His jersey is often seen worn by fans at Bears' games, reflecting his enduring legacy.
- Luckman was known for his quick release, making it hard for defenders to sack him.
- He had a close relationship with owner and coach George Halas.
- Sid was a trendsetter, laying the foundation for future great quarterbacks.
- He remains a symbol of excellence in quarterback play.
- Luckman was a team player, often deflecting praise to his teammates.
- He's remembered not only for his on-field achievements but also for his character and leadership.

Red Grange

- Red Grange was born on June 13, 1903, in Forksville, Pennsylvania.
- He was one of the NFL's first big stars, earning the nickname "The Galloping Ghost."
- Grange played for the Bears in two stints, from 1925 to 1926 and then from 1929 to 1934.
- Before his pro career, he was a standout at the University of Illinois.
- His number, 77, was retired by the Chicago Bears.
- He was a charter member of both the College Football Hall of Fame and the Pro Football Hall of Fame.
- Red's college exploits included a famous game where he scored four touchdowns in 12 minutes.
- His signing with the Bears led to a significant surge in the league's popularity.
- He played halfback and was known for his incredible speed and elusive running style.
- Grange's barnstorming tour with the Bears in 1925 is legendary, playing in 19 games in 67 days.
- He also had a brief career in film and radio.
- Red Grange served as an assistant coach for the Bears after his playing days.
- He also had a successful career as a sports announcer.
- His collegiate career saw him earn three All-America honors.
- Grange was the first recipient of the Chicago Tribune Silver Football award, given to the Big Ten's most valuable player.
- He is often credited with legitimizing the NFL due to his star power.
- Red's NFL debut drew an estimated 36,000 fans, a testament to his drawing power.
- He played in the first-ever game at Wrigley Field.
- His career was briefly interrupted due to a dispute with George Halas, leading him to play for the New York Yankees football team.
- Grange suffered a severe knee injury in 1927, which hampered his career.
- Despite this, he returned to the Bears and continued to be a significant player for them.

- He played in the first-ever NFL Championship game in 1932.
- Grange's impact extended beyond the field, making significant contributions to the game's business side.
- He was known for his humility and was revered by both teammates and opponents.
- His contributions to football have been immortalized in literature, film, and music.
- Grange passed away on January 28, 1991.
- He remains one of the most iconic figures in the history of American sports.
- Red was a multi-sport athlete, also excelling in baseball and track and field.
- He scored a total of 31 touchdowns during his NFL career.
- Grange was also a successful businessman, owning an insurance company.
- He was known for his incredible vision on the field, often seeing plays develop before they happened.
- Red's college games often saw him outpacing entire teams, leading to legendary status.
- His influence led to significant growth in the NFL's fanbase during the league's early years.
- He was part of an era where players often played both offense and defense.
- Grange's style of play often left crowds in awe, leading to his enduring legacy.
- His endurance was also legendary, often playing entire games without rest.
- Red's name is synonymous with the "Golden Age" of sports in the 1920s.
- His fame transcended football, making him one of the most recognized personalities of his time.
- He was known for his fair play and sportsmanship.
- His college exploits at Illinois are still celebrated, with the university honoring him in various ways.
- Grange was a significant figure in establishing the running back position's importance in football.
- He was known for his ability to change the game's momentum with a single play.
- Red was one of the first athletes to have a manager and agent.

- His decision to turn pro immediately after college was controversial at the time but changed the game.
- Grange's battles against Jim Thorpe's Canton Bulldogs are stuff of legends.
- He remains an essential figure in discussions about the greatest football players of all time.
- His influence in popularizing the NFL cannot be overstated.
- Grange's jersey remains a popular item among fans and collectors.
- He had a significant impact on how the game was marketed and presented to the public.
- Red Grange's legacy is that of an athlete who changed the face of professional football.

Justin Fields

- Justin Fields was born on March 5, 1999, in Kennesaw, Georgia.
- The Chicago Bears drafted him in the first round of the 2021 NFL Draft.
- Before joining the NFL, Fields played college football for Georgia and Ohio State.
- At Ohio State, he was a Heisman Trophy finalist.
- Fields is known for his dual-threat capabilities, both as a passer and a runner.
- In college, he threw 67 touchdowns and ran for 15 more.
- Justin played a crucial role in leading Ohio State to the College Football Playoff.
- He's known for his strong arm and accuracy.
- In the 2021 NFL draft, he was the 11th overall pick.
- Fields played a pivotal role in a famous win over Clemson in the CFP semi-final, throwing six touchdowns.
- He's been praised for his work ethic and dedication.
- Justin began his college career at the University of Georgia before transferring to Ohio State.
- He has been active in advocating for player rights and social justice causes.
- Fields was instrumental in the Big Ten's decision to play football in the COVID-19 affected 2020 season.
- In his debut season with Ohio State, he was named Big Ten Offensive Player of the Year.
- He earned a reputation in college for his ability to perform in big games.
- Fields is seen as a vital part of the Bears' future, with fans and analysts excited about his potential.
- He's also known for his speed, recording a 4.44-second 40-yard dash.
- Justin is known to be a diligent student of the game, often spending hours studying playbooks.
- He played a total of 22 games for Ohio State over two seasons.
- Fields made his NFL debut for the Bears against the Los Angeles Rams.
- He's the highest-drafted quarterback by the Bears since Mitchell Trubisky in 2017.

- Justin has shown resilience, often bouncing back from tough games with standout performances.
- He's known for his leadership qualities, earning respect from teammates early in his career.
- Fields had a standout game against Michigan in 2019, throwing for 302 yards and 4 touchdowns.
- He's been active in community work and charity initiatives.
- Justin is known for his poise under pressure, often delivering in clutch moments.
- He played baseball in high school and was good enough to be considered for college baseball.
- Fields has a strong relationship with his family, often crediting them for his success.
- He's been praised by coaches for his quick decision-making on the field.
- Justin's college jersey number was 1, which he continued with the Bears.
- He has shown the ability to make plays outside the pocket, often extending plays with his legs.
- Fields is seen as a player around whom the Bears can build their team for the future.
- He's been open about his journey and challenges, endearing him to fans.
- Justin played in some of the biggest games in college football, including the Rose Bowl.
- His performance against the Clemson Tigers in 2020, where he threw six touchdowns, is considered one of the best in college playoff history.
- Fields is part of a new generation of NFL quarterbacks known for their versatility.
- He's been an advocate for player safety and mental health.
- Justin's determination was evident when he played through a significant rib injury in college.
- He's seen as a role model for young players, especially those looking to make the transition from college to the NFL.
- Fields has expressed his excitement and commitment to bringing success to the Bears.
- His journey from Georgia to Ohio State and then to the NFL has been closely followed by the media.

● Justin has shown maturity beyond his years, handling media scrutiny with grace.

● He's known for his competitive spirit, often pushing himself and his teammates to be better.

● Fields has a bright future, with many expecting him to be among the NFL's elite quarterbacks.

● He's also known for his camaraderie with teammates, building strong relationships.

● Justin has shown adaptability, transitioning from two major college programs and adjusting to the NFL's rigors.

● His footwork and mechanics have been praised by coaches and analysts alike.

● Fields is seen as a game-changer, with the ability to turn games around with his performances.

● He represents hope and excitement for the Chicago Bears and their fanbase, eager to see him lead the team to success.

Mike Singletary

- Mike Singletary was born on October 9, 1958, in Houston, Texas.
  - He played college football at Baylor University.
  - At Baylor, he was a two-time All-American.
  - Singletary was known for his intense focus and piercing gaze during games.
  - He was drafted by the Chicago Bears in the 2nd round of the 1981 NFL Draft.
  - Quickly became the anchor of the Bears' defense.
  - Earned the nickname "Samurai Mike" due to his fierce style of play.
  - Key player for the Bears when they won Super Bowl XX in 1986.
  - Named the NFL Defensive Player of the Year twice, in 1985 and 1988.
  - A 10-time Pro Bowl selection during his career.
  - Played his entire 12-season NFL career with the Bears.
  - In total, he recorded 1,488 tackles, 19 sacks, and 7 interceptions.
  - Known for his leadership on and off the field.
  - Inducted into the Pro Football Hall of Fame in 1998.
  - Became a coach after his playing career.
  - Had a stint as the head coach of the San Francisco 49ers.
  - The Bears retired his jersey number, 50.
  - A devout Christian.
  - Often spoke about the influence of his faith on his life and career.
  - Known for rigorous preparation, often watching hours of film.
  - Was a critical part of the '85 Bears defense, which is considered one of the best in NFL history.
  - Married Kim Singletary, and together they have seven children.
  - Co-authored several books during and after his career.
  - Has also been involved in various charitable endeavors.
  - In 2003, he joined the Baltimore Ravens as a linebackers coach.
  - Was known for his incredible work ethic during his playing days.
  - Consistently praised by his coaches for his dedication to the game.
  - Mike's fiery speeches and pep talks were legendary in the locker room.
  - Was known to mentor younger players and help them adjust to the league.

- Played alongside other legendary players like Walter Payton and Jim McMahon.
- Despite his fierce demeanor on the field, he was well-respected and well-liked by teammates and opponents alike.
- Has said that his biggest inspiration was his father, who taught him the value of hard work.
- Considered one of the best middle linebackers in NFL history.
- Known for his ability to diagnose plays before they happened.
- Often credited with changing the way the middle linebacker position was played.
- Was the first rookie to lead the Bears in tackles since 1975.
- Recorded a career-high 13 tackles in a game on three separate occasions.
- Was the Bears' team captain for most of his career.
- Finished his career with 10 fumble recoveries.
- Was a member of the 1980s All-Decade Team.
- Was always approachable to fans and often signed autographs.
- Featured in several commercials and TV shows during his playing career.
- Has always credited his coaches for his success, especially Buddy Ryan.
- Became an inspiration for future linebackers like Ray Lewis and Brian Urlacher.
- Was often described as the "heart and soul" of the Bears' defense.
- Earned respect not just for his play but also for playing through injuries.
- Was considered a "student of the game" for his detailed note-taking and film study.
- Is often remembered for his iconic stare-downs with opposing quarterbacks.
- Led the Bears in tackles in eight of his 12 seasons.
- Was the defensive signal-caller for the Bears, responsible for communicating plays and adjustments.

Brian Urlacher

- Brian Urlacher was born on May 25, 1978, in Pasco, Washington.
  - Played college football at the University of New Mexico.
  - Recognized in college for his versatility, playing both linebacker and safety.
  - Drafted by the Chicago Bears with the 9th overall pick in the 2000 NFL Draft.
  - Named the NFL Defensive Rookie of the Year in 2000.
  - Known for his speed, athleticism, and ability to read the game.
  - An 8-time Pro Bowl selection during his career.
  - Named the NFL Defensive Player of the Year in 2005.
  - The face of the Bears' defense for over a decade.
  - Recorded over 1,300 tackles, 41.5 sacks, and 22 interceptions.
  - Inducted into the Pro Football Hall of Fame in 2018.
  - Known for his iconic bald head.
  - Played his entire 13-season NFL career with the Bears.
  - The Bears retired his jersey number, 54.
  - Known for his community involvement.
  - Often participated in charity events in Chicago.
  - Grew up in Lovington, New Mexico, and has spoken about the influence of his upbringing on his work ethic.
  - Was a state-recognized high school player in multiple sports including football, basketball, and track.
  - In college, he was the star of the New Mexico Lobos, setting multiple school records.
  - Was initially viewed as a safety in the NFL but the Bears saw his potential at linebacker.
  - Became a fan favorite in Chicago due to his relentless play and likable personality.
  - Was a significant part of the Bears' 2006 team that went to Super Bowl XLI.
  - Despite his on-field intensity, he was known for his jovial and light-hearted nature off the field.
  - Appeared in numerous commercials, often poking fun at himself.

- Established the Brian Urlacher Foundation, which supports underprivileged children.
- Has four children and has spoken about the joys and challenges of fatherhood.
- After retirement, he became an analyst for Fox Sports 1.
- His number, 54, became synonymous with the Bears' defensive excellence during his tenure.
- Was known for his ability to drop into coverage, a rarity for middle linebackers of his size.
- Often credited with revitalizing the Bears' defense in the 2000s.
- Was teammates with other Bear legends like Lance Briggs and Charles Tillman.
- His athleticism was showcased when he famously chased down Michael Vick, one of the fastest quarterbacks in NFL history.
- Earned respect across the league, with many players naming him as one of the toughest opponents they faced.
- Was the NFL's Alumni Linebacker of the Year in 2005.
- Finished his career with 22 interceptions, an impressive number for a middle linebacker.
- Often credited his success to his coaches and teammates.
- Known for his ability to rally his team, both with his play and his leadership.
- His Hall of Fame induction ceremony was attended by thousands of Bears fans, showcasing his impact on the fanbase.
- Despite facing multiple injuries, he only missed significant time in two of his thirteen seasons.
- Known for his impressive vertical leap, often batting down passes at the line of scrimmage.
- Is often cited as an example of how to transition smoothly from a playing career to a media career.
- Known for his iconic "Urlacher shuffle" celebration after big plays.
- Was named to the NFL 2000s All-Decade Team.
- His rivalry with Packers quarterback Brett Favre was one of the highlights of the NFL during the early 2000s.

● Is often remembered for his humility, always deflecting praise onto his teammates.

● Was known for his rigorous off-season training regimen.

● Despite his many accolades, he always spoke of his regret of not winning a Super Bowl.

● Was the Bears' team captain for the majority of his career.

● Known for his close relationship with the Chicago community, often giving back through charitable endeavors.

● His legacy as one of the best linebackers in NFL history is solidified, not just by stats, but by his impact on the game.

Richard Dent

- Richard Dent was born on December 13, 1960, in Atlanta, Georgia.
- Played college football at Tennessee State University, a historically black university.
- Drafted in the 8th round of the 1983 NFL Draft by the Chicago Bears.
- A key player in the Bears' Super Bowl XX victory.
- Named Super Bowl XX MVP.
- Over his career, Dent recorded 137.5 sacks.
- Known for his ability to rush the passer.
- Incredible speed for a defensive end.
- A 4-time Pro Bowl selection.
- Played 15 seasons in the NFL.
- Inducted into the Pro Football Hall of Fame in 2011.
- Also played for the 49ers, Colts, and Eagles.
- Most associated with the Bears.
- A key member of the Bears' iconic 1985 defense.
- Wore jersey number 95 with the Bears.
- Known for his quiet demeanor off the field.
- Fierce competitiveness on the field.
- His underdog story is an inspiration.
- Despite being a late-round draft pick, he rose to be one of the greats.
- Was known to use his hands effectively to fend off offensive linemen.
- His sack dance celebration was iconic in the 80s.
- Led the NFC in sacks in 1984 with 17.5.
- His partnership with other Bears' defensive legends like Mike Singletary was pivotal in the team's success.
- Became a successful businessman after his playing career.
- Was a vocal advocate for players' rights, especially post-career health benefits.
- Credited his college coach Joe Gilliam Sr. for his development as a player.
- Despite his successes, always remained humble.
- Known to mentor younger players during his career.
- His spin move was feared by offensive tackles.

- Played in 203 NFL games, starting 151 of them.
- His 34 forced fumbles are a testament to his playmaking ability.
- Was known to study opposing offensive linemen to understand their tendencies.
- Despite his many sacks, he also was stout against the run.
- Was named the NFC Defensive Player of the Month in October 1984.
- His battles with NFC Central offensive linemen were legendary.
- Always credited his teammates for his individual success.
- Returned to the Bears in 1995 after stints with other teams.
- Retired as a Bear in 1997.
- Was known for his leadership, especially in big games.
- His 8 postseason sacks are a testament to his ability to perform in clutch situations.
- Was a key voice in the locker room, especially during the Bears' Super Bowl run.
- Despite facing numerous double teams, his production never dipped.
- Is remembered for his iconic game against the Redskins in 1984, where he recorded 3.5 sacks.
- His combination of size and speed was rare during his playing days.
- Despite facing multiple injuries, always found a way to contribute.
- Was a team-first player, often playing through pain.
- Was known for his extensive charity work in Chicago.
- Is often regarded as one of the best draft steals in NFL history.
- Has spoken about the influence of his mother on his work ethic.
- Despite his on-field dominance, he is remembered as a gentle giant off the field.

Don't miss out!

Visit the website below and you can sign up to receive emails whenever Trivia Ape publishes a new book. There's no charge and no obligation.

https://books2read.com/r/B-A-CUAAB-IPENC

Connecting independent readers to independent writers.

Did you love *Chicago Bears Fun Facts*? Then you should read *Pittsburgh Steelers Fun Facts*[1] by Trivia Ape!

Discover the ultimate fan experience with the "Pittsburgh Steelers Fun Facts" book – an exciting journey through the rich history and legendary moments of this iconic NFL team. Packed with over 1000 detailed fun facts, this family-friendly book is designed to challenge and entertain fans of all ages while deepening their knowledge of the Pittsburgh Steelers.

Immerse yourself in the heart-pounding action, unforgettable plays, and standout players that have defined their legacy. From thrilling rivalries and historic divisional matchups to legendary offensive star players and iconic stadium facts, each question provides a captivating glimpse into the team's remarkable journey.

Unearth captivating insights into the team origins, relive iconic victories, and celebrate the achievements of Hall of Fame players who have graced the field for this epic franchise. With a careful balance of challenging facts and accessible

1. https://books2read.com/u/mYqyLV

2. https://books2read.com/u/mYqyLV

content, readers will learn fascinating facts, engage in spirited discussions, and proudly display their Pittsburgh Steelers expertise.

Whether you're a lifelong fan looking to increase your knowledge or a newcomer eager to learn about their storied past, the "Pittsburgh Steelers Fun Facts" book is your go-to source for immersive entertainment.

Also by Trivia Ape

50 States Trivia
Kansas City Chiefs Trivia Book
Chicago Bears Fun Facts
Green Bay Packers Fun Facts
Kansas City Chiefs Fun Facts
Minnesota Vikings Fun Facts
Denver Broncos Fun Facts
Detroit Lions Fun Facts
Las Vegas Raiders Fun Facts
Los Angeles Chargers Fun Facts
Pittsburgh Steelers Fun Facts

www.ingramcontent.com/pod-product-compliance
Lightning Source LLC
Chambersburg PA
CBHW061334120726
48001CB00002B/857